W. E. Gladstone

The Vatican Decrees In Their Bearing On Civil Allegiance

A Political Expostulation

W. E. Gladstone

The Vatican Decrees In Their Bearing On Civil Allegiance
A Political Expostulation

ISBN/EAN: 9783337080761

Printed in Europe, USA, Canada, Australia, Japan

Cover: Foto ©Suzi / pixelio.de

More available books at **www.hansebooks.com**

THE VATICAN DECREES

IN THEIR BEARING ·ON

CIVIL ALLEGIANCE:

A POLITICAL EXPOSTULATION.

BY THE

RIGHT HON. W. E. GLADSTONE, M.P.

LONDON:

JOHN MURRAY, ALBEMARLE STREET.

1874.

LONDON :

PRINTED BY WILLIAM CLOWES AND SONS,

STAMFORD STREET AND CHARING CROSS.

CONTENTS.

THE VATICAN DECREES

IN THEIR BEARING ON

CIVIL ALLEGIANCE.

I. The Occasion and Scope of this Tract.

In the prosecution of a purpose not polemical but
pacific, I have been led to employ words which belong,
more or less, to the region of religious controversy;
and which, though they were themselves few, seem to
require, from the various feelings they have aroused,
that I should carefully define, elucidate, and defend
them. The task is not of a kind agreeable to me;
but I proceed to perform it.

Among the causes, which have tended to disturb
and perplex the public mind in the consideration of
our own religious difficulties, one has been a certain
alarm at the aggressive activity and imagined growth
of the Roman Church in this country. All are aware
of our susceptibility on this side; and it was not, I
think, improper for one who desires to remove everything that can interfere with a calm and judicial
temper, and who believes the alarm to be groundless,

to state, pointedly though briefly, some reasons for that belief.

Accordingly I did not scruple to use the following language, in a paper inserted in the number of the Contemporary Review' for the month of October. I was speaking of "the question whether a handful of the clergy are or are not engaged in an utterly hopeless and visionary effort to Romanise the Church and people of England."

"At no time since the bloody reign of Mary has such a scheme been possible. But if it had been possible in the seventeenth or eighteenth centuries, it would still have become impossible in the nineteenth : when Rome has substituted for the proud boast of *semper eadem* a policy of violence and change in faith ; when she has refurbished, and paraded anew, every rusty tool she was fondly thought to have disused ; when no one.can become her convert without renouncing his moral and mental freedom, and placing his civil loyalty and duty at the mercy of another ; and when she has equally repudiated modern thought and ancient history."*

Had I been, when I wrote this passage, as I now am, addressing myself in considerable measure to my Roman Catholic fellow-countrymen, I should have striven to avoid the seeming roughness of some of these expressions ; but as the question is now about

---

Contemporary Review,' Oct. 1874, p. 674.

their substance, from which I am not in any particular disposed to recede, any attempt to recast their general form would probably mislead. I proceed, then, to deal with them on their merits.

More than one friend of mine, among those who have been led to join the Roman Catholic communion, has made this passage the subject, more or less, of expostulation. Now, in my opinion, the assertions which it makes are, as coming from a layman who has spent most and the best years of his life in the observation and practice of politics, not aggressive but defensive.

It is neither the abettors of the Papal Chair, nor any one who, however far from being an abettor of the Papal Chair, actually writes from a Papal point of view, that has a right to remonstrate with the world at large; but it is the world at large, on the contrary, that has the fullest right to remonstrate, first with His Holiness, secondly with those who share his proceedings, thirdly even with such as passively allow and accept them.

I therefore, as one of the world at large, propose to expostulate in my turn. I shall strive to show to such of my Roman Catholic fellow-subjects as may kindly give me a hearing that, after the singular steps which the authorities of their Church have in these last years thought fit to take, the people of this country, who fully believe in their loyalty, are entitled, on purely civil grounds, to expect from them some declaration or manifestation of opinion, in reply to that ecclesiastical party in their Church who have laid down, in their name, principles adverse to the purity and integrity of civil allegiance.

Undoubtedly my allegations are of great breadth. Such broad allegations require a broad and a deep foundation. The first question which they raise is, Are they, as to the material part of them, true? But even their truth might not suffice to show that their publication was opportune. The second question, then, which they raise is, Are they, for any practical purpose, material? And there is yet a third, though a minor, question, which arises out of the propositions in connection with their authorship, Were they suitable to be set forth by the present writer?

To these three questions I will now set myself to reply. And the matter of my reply will, as I conceive, constitute and convey an appeal to the understandings of my Roman Catholic fellow-countrymen, which I trust that, at the least, some among them may deem not altogether unworthy of their consideration.

From the language used by some of the organs of Roman Catholic opinion, it is, I am afraid, plain that in some quarters they have given deep offence. Displeasure, indignation, even fury, might be said to mark the language which in the heat of the moment has been expressed here and there. They have been hastily treated as an attack made upon Roman Catholics generally, nay, as an insult offered them. It is obvious to reply, that of Roman Catholics generally they state nothing. Together with a reference to "converts," of which I shall say more, they constitute generally a free and strong animadversion on the conduct of the Papal Chair, and of its advisers and abettors. If I am told that he who animadverts upon these assails thereby, or insults, Roman Catholics at large, who do not choose their ecclesiastical rulers, and are not recognised as having any voice in the government of their Church, I cannot be bound by or accept a proposition which seems to me to be so little in accordance with reason.

Before all things, however, I should desire it to be understood that, in the remarks now offered, I desire to eschew not only religious bigotry, but likewise theological controversy. Indeed, with theology, except in its civil bearing, with theology as such, I have here nothing whatever to do. But it is the peculiarity of Roman theology that, by thrusting itself into the temporal domain, it naturally, and even necessarily, comes to be a frequent theme of political discussion. To quiet-minded Roman Catholics, it must be a subject of infinite annoyance, that their religion is, on this ground more than any other, the subject of criticism; more than any other, the occasion of conflicts with the State and of civil disquietude. I feel sincerely how much hardship their case entails. But this hardship is brought upon them altogether by the conduct of the authorities of their own Church.

Why did theology enter so largely into the debates
of Parliament on Roman Catholic Emancipation?
Certainly not because our statesmen and debaters of
fifty years ago had an abstract love of such controversies, but because it was extensively believed that
the Pope of Rome had been and was a trespasser upon
ground which belonged to the civil authority, and that
he affected to determine by spiritual prerogative questions of the civil sphere. This fact, if fact it be, and
not the truth or falsehood, the reasonableness or
unreasonableness, of any article of purely religious
belief, is the whole and sole cause of the mischief.
To this fact, and to this fact alone, my language
is referable : but for this fact, it would have been
neither my duty nor my desire to use it. All other
Christian bodies are content with freedom in their
own religious domain. Orientals, Lutherans, Cal-
vinists, Presbyterians, Episcopalians, Nonconformists,
one and all, in the present day, contentedly and
thankfully accept the benefits of civil order; never
pretend that the State is not its own master; make
no religious claims to temporal possessions or advan-
tages ; and, consequently, never are in perilous collision with the State. Nay more, even so I believe
it is with the mass of Roman Catholics individually.
But not so with the leaders of their Church, or with
those who take pride in following the leaders.
Indeed, this has been made matter of boast :—

" There is not another Church so called " (than the Roman),

" nor any community professing to be a Church, which does not submit, or obey, or hold its peace, when the civil governors of the world command."—' The Present Crisis of the Holy See,' by H. E. Manning, D.D. London, 1861, p. 75.

The Rome of the Middle Ages claimed universal monarchy. The modern Church of Rome has abandoned nothing, retracted nothing. Is that all? Far from it. By condemning (as will be seen) those who, like Bishop Doyle in 1826,* charge the mediæval Popes with aggression, she unconditionally, even if covertly, maintains what the mediæval Popes maintained. But even this is not the worst. The worst by far is that whereas, in the national Churches and communities of the Middle Ages, there was a brisk, vigorous, and constant opposition to these outrageous claims, an opposition which stoutly asserted its own orthodoxy, which always caused itself to be respected, and which even sometimes gained the upper hand; now, in this nineteenth century of ours, and while it is growing old, this same opposition has been put out of court, and judicially extinguished within the Papal Church, by the recent decrees of the Vatican. And it is impossible for persons accepting those decrees justly to complain, when such documents are subjected in good faith to a strict examination as respects their compatibility with civil right and the obedience of subjects.

---

* Lords' Committee, March 18, 1826. Report, p. 190.

In defending my language, I shall carefully mark its limits. But all defence is reassertion, which properly requires a deliberate reconsideration; and no man who thus reconsiders should scruple, if he find so much as a word that may convey a false impression, to amend it. Exactness in stating truth according to the measure of our intelligence, is an indispensable condition of justice, and of a title to be heard.

My propositions, then, as they stood, are these :—

1. That " Rome has substituted for the proud boast of *semper eadem*, a policy of violence and change in faith."

2. That she has refurbished and paraded anew every rusty tool she was fondly thought to have disused.

3. That no one can now become her convert without renouncing his moral and mental freedom, and placing his civil loyalty and duty at the mercy of another.

4. That she (" Rome ") has equally repudiated modern thought and ancient history.

II. The First and the Fourth Propositions.

Of the first and fourth of these propositions I shall dispose rather summarily, as they appear to belong to the theological domain. They refer to a fact, and they record an opinion. One fact to which they

refer is this : that, in days within my memory, the
constant, favourite, and imposing argument of Roman
controversialists was the unbroken and absolute
identity in belief of the Roman Church from the
days of our Saviour until now. No one, who has at
all followed the course of this literature during the
last forty years, can fail to be sensible of the change
in its present tenour. More and more have the
assertions of continuous uniformity of doctrine re-
ceded into scarcely penetrable shadow. More and
more have another series of assertions, of a living
authority, ever ready to open, adopt, and shape
Christian doctrine according to the times, taken their
place. Without discussing the abstract compatibility
of these lines of argument, I note two of the immense
practical differences between them. In the first, the
office claimed by the Church is principally that of a witness to facts ; in the second, principally that of a judge,
if not a revealer, of doctrine. In the first, the processes
which the Church undertakes are subject to a constant challenge and appeal to history ; in the second,
no amount of historical testimony can avail against
the unmeasured power of the theory of develop-
ment. Most important, most pregnant considerations, these, at least for two classes of persons: for
those who think that exaggerated doctrines of Church
power are among the real and serious dangers of the
age ; and for those who think that against all forms,
both of superstition and of unbelief, one main pre-

servative is to be found in maintaining the truth and authority of history, and the inestimable value of the historic spirit.

So much for the fact; as for the opinion, that the recent Papal decrees are at war with modern thought, and that, purporting to enlarge the necessary creed of Christendom, they involve a violent breach with history, this is a matter unfit for me to discuss, as it is a question of Divinity ; but not unfit for me to have mentioned in my article; since the opinion given there is the opinion of those with whom I was endeavouring to reason, namely, the great majority of the British public.

If it is thought that the word violence was open to exception, I regret I cannot give it up. The justification of the ancient definitions of the Church, which have endured the storms of 1500 years, was to be found in this, that they were not arbitrary or wilful, but that they wholly sprang from, and related to theories rampant at the time, and regarded as menacing to Christian belief. Even the Canons of the Council of Trent have in the main this amount, apart from their matter, of presumptive warrant. But the decrees of the present perilous Pontificate have been passed to favour and precipitate prevailing currents of opinion in the ecclesiastical world of Rome. The growth of what is often termed among Protestants Mariolatry, and of belief in Papal Infallibility, was notoriously advancing, but it seems not fast enough to satisfy the dominant party. To aim the deadly blows of 1854* and 1870 at the old historic, scientific, and moderate school, was surely an act of violence ; and with this censure the proceeding of 1870 has actually been visited by the first living theologian now within the Roman Communion, I mean, Dr. John Henry Newman ; who has used these significant words, among others : " Why should an aggressive and insolent faction be allowed to make the heart of the just sad, whom the Lord hath not made sorrowful ?" †

III. THE SECOND PROPOSITION.

I take next my second Proposition : that Rome has refurbished, and paraded anew, every rusty tool she was fondly thought to have disused.

Is this then a fact, or is it not?

I must assume that it is denied ; and therefore I cannot wholly pass by the work of proof. But I will state in the fewest possible words, and with references, a few propositions, all the holders of which have been *condemned* by the See of Rome during my own generation, and especially within the last twelve or fifteen years. And, in order that I may do nothing towards importing passion into what is matter of

---

* Decree of the Immaculate Conception.

† See the remarkable Letter of Dr. Newman to Bishop Ullathorne, in the ' Guardian ' of April 6. 1870.

pure argument, I will avoid citing any of the fearfully energetic epithets in which the condemnations are sometimes clothed.

1. Those who maintain the Liberty of the Press. Encyclical Letter of Pope Gregory XVI., in 1831: and of Pope Pius IX., in 1864.

2. Or the liberty of conscience and of worship. Encyclical of Pius IX., December 8, 1864.

3. Or the liberty of speech. 'Syllabus' of March 18, 1861. Prop. lxxix. Encyclical of Pope Pius IX., December 8, 1864.

4. Or who contend that Papal judgments and decrees may, without sin, be disobeyed, or differed from, unless they treat of the rules (*dogmata*) of faith or morals. Ibid.

5. Or who assign to the State the power of defining the civil rights (*jura*) and province of the Church. 'Syllabus' of Pope Pius IX., December 8, 1864. Ibid. Prop. xix.

6. Or who hold that Roman Pontiffs and Ecumenical Councils have transgressed the limits of their power, and usurped the rights of princes. Ibid. Prop. xxiii.

(*It must be borne in mind, that " Ecumenical Councils " here mean Roman Councils, not recognised by the rest of the Church. The Councils of the early Church did not interfere with the jurisdiction of the civil power.*)

7. Or that the Church may not employ force.

(*Ecclesia vis inferendæ potestatem non habet.*) ' Syllabus,' Prop. xxiv.

8. Or that power, not inherent in the office of the Episcopate, but granted to it by the civil authority, may be withdrawn from it at the discretion of that authority.   Ibid. Prop. xxv.

9. Or that the civil immunity (*immunitas*) of the Church and its ministers, depends upon civil right. Ibid. Prop. xxx.

10. Or that in the conflict of laws civil and ecclesiastical, the civil law should prevail.   Ibid. Prop. xlii.

11. Or that any method of instruction of youth, solely secular, may be approved.   Ibid. Prop. xlviii.

12. Or that knowledge of things philosophical and civil, may and should decline to be guided by Divine *and Ecclesiastical* authority.   Ibid. Prop. lvii.

13. Or that marriage is not in its essence a Sacrament.   Ibid. Prop. lxvi.

14. Or that marriage, not sacramentally contracted, (*si sacramentum excludatur*) has a binding force.   Ibid. Prop. lxxiii.

15. Or that the abolition of the Temporal Power of the Popedom would be highly advantageous to the Church.   Ibid. Prop. lxxvi.   Also lxx.

16. Or that any other religion than the Roman religion may be established by a State.   Ibid. Prop. lxxvii.

17. Or that in " Countries called Catholic," the

free exerciso of other religions may laudably be allowed. ' Syllabus,' Prop. lxxviii.

18. Or that the Roman Pontiff ought to come to terms with progress, liberalism, and modern civilization. Ibid. Prop. lxxx. *

This list is now perhaps sufficiently extended, although I have as yet not touched the decrees of 1870. But, before quitting it, I must offer three observations on what it contains.

Firstly. I do not place all the Propositions in one and the same category ; for there are a portion of them which, as far as I can judge, might, by the combined aid of favourable construction and vigorous explanation, be brought within bounds. And I hold that favourable construction of the terms used in controversies is the right general rule. But this can only be so, when construction is an open question. When the author of certain propositions claims, as in the case before us, a sole and unlimited power to interpret them in such manner and by such rules as he may from time to time think fit, the only defence for all others concerned is at once to judge for themselves, how much of unreason or of mischief the words, naturally understood, may contain.

Secondly. It may appear, upon a hasty perusal, that neither the infliction of penalty in life, limb,

---

* For the original passages from the Encyclical and Syllabus of Pius IX., see Appendix A.

liberty, or goods, on disobedient members of the
Christian Church, nor the title to depose sovereigns,
and release subjects from their allegiance, with all its
revolting consequences, has been here reaffirmed. In
terms, there is no mention of them ; but in the substance of the propositions, I grieve to say, they are
beyond doubt included. For it is notorious that they
have been declared and decreed by " Rome," that is
to say by Popes and Papal Councils ; and the stringent
condemnations of the Syllabus include all those who
hold that Popes and Papal Councils (declared ecumenical) have transgressed the just limits of their power,
or usurped the rights of princes. What have been
their opinions and decrees about persecution I need
hardly say ; and indeed the right to employ physical
force is even here undisguisedly claimed (No. 7).

Even while I am writing, I am reminded, from an
unquestionable source, of the words of Pope Pius IX.
himself on the deposing power. I add only a few
italics; the words appear as given in a translation,
without the original :—

" The present Pontiff used these words in replying to the
address from the Academia of the Catholic Religion (July 21,
1873) :—

" ' There are many errors regarding the Infallibility : but the
most malicious of all is that which includes, in that dogma, the
right of deposing sovereigns, and declaring the people no longer
bound by the obligation of fidelity. This *right* has now and
again, in critical circumstances, been exercised by the Pontiffs :
but it has nothing to do with Papal Infallibility. Its origin was
not the infallibility, but the authority of the Pope. This

authority, in accordance with public right, which was then vigorous, and with the acquiescence of all Christian nations, who reverenced in the Pope the supreme Judge of the Christian Commonwealth, *extended so far as to pass judgment, even in civil affairs, on the acts of Princes and of Nations.'* " *

Lastly. I must observe that these are not mere opinions of the Pope himself, nor even are they opinions which he might paternally recommend to the pious consideration of the faithful. With the promulgation of his opinions is unhappily combined, in the Encyclical Letter, which virtually, though not expressly, includes the whole, a command to all his spiritual children (from which command we the disobedient children are in no way excluded) to hold them.

"Itaque omnes et singulas pravas opiniones et doctrinas singillatim hisce literis commemoratas auctoritate nostrâ Apostolicâ reprobamus, proscribimus, atque damnamus; easque ab omnibus Catholicæ Ecclesiæ filiis, veluti reprobatas, proscriptas, atque damnatas omnino haberi volumus et mandamus" (a). Encycl. Dec. 8, 1864.

And the decrees of 1870 will presently show us, what they establish as the binding force of the *mandate* thus conveyed to the Christian world.

----

* 'Civilization and the See of Rome.' By Lord Robert Montagu. Dublin, 1874. A Lecture delivered under the auspices of the Catholic Union of Ireland. I have a little misgiving about the version: but not of a nature to affect the substance.

(a) For translation of this passage, see p. 71.

IV. THE THIRD PROPOSITION.

I now pass to the operation of these extraordinary declarations on personal and private duty.

When the cup of endurance, which had so long been filling, began, with the council of the Vatican in 1870, to overflow, the most famous and learned living theologian of the Roman Communion, Dr. von Döllinger, long the foremost champion of his Church, refused compliance, and submitted, with his temper undisturbed and his freedom unimpaired, to the extreme and most painful penalty of excommunication. With him, many of the most learned and respected theologians of the Roman Communion in Germany underwent the same sentence. The very few, who elsewhere (I do not speak of Switzerland) suffered in like manner, deserve an admiration rising in proportion to their fewness. It seems as though Germany, from which Luther blew the mighty trumpet that even now echoes through the land, still retained her primacy in the domain of conscience, still supplied the *centuria prærogativa* of the great *comitia* of the world.

But let no man wonder or complain. Without imputing to anyone the moral murder, for such it is, of stifling conscience and conviction, I for one cannot be surprised that the fermentation, which is working through the mind of the Latin Church, has as yet (elsewhere than in Germany) but in few instances come to the surface. By the mass of mankind, it is

morally impossible that questions such as these can
be adequately examined; so it ever has been, and so
in the main it will continue, until the principles of
manufacturing machinery shall have been applied,
and with analogous results, to intellectual and moral
processes. Followers they are and must be, and in a
certain sense ought to be. But what as to the leaders
of society, the men of education and of leisure ? I will
try to suggest some answer in few words. A change of
religious profession is under all circumstances a great
and awful thing. Much more is the question, however,
between conflicting, or apparently conflicting, duties
arduous, when the religion of a man has been changed
for him, over his head, and without the very least of
his participation. Far be it then from me to make any
Roman Catholic, except the great hierarchic Power,
and those who have egged it on, responsible for the
portentous proceedings which we have witnessed.
My conviction is that, even of those who may not shake
off the yoke, multitudes will vindicate at any rate their
loyalty at the expense of the consistency, which perhaps in difficult matters of religion few among us perfectly maintain. But this belongs to the future ; for
the present, nothing could in my opinion be more
unjust than to hold the members of the Roman Church
in general already responsible for the recent innova-
tions. The duty of observers, who think the claims
involved in these decrees arrogant and false, and such
as not even impotence real or supposed ought to

shield from criticism, is frankly to state the case, and, by way of friendly challenge, to intreat their Roman Catholic fellow-countrymen to replace themselves in the position which five-and-forty years ago this nation, by the voice and action of its Parliament, declared its belief that they held.

Upon a strict re-examination of the language, as a part from the substance of my fourth Proposition, I find it faulty, inasmuch as it seems to imply that a "convert" now joining the Papal Church, not only gives up certain rights and duties of freedom, but surrenders them by a conscious and deliberate act. What I have less accurately said that he renounced, I might have more accurately said that he forfeited. To speak strictly, the claim now made upon him by the authority, which he solemnly and with the highest responsibility acknowledges, requires him to surrender his mental and moral freedom, and to place his loyalty and civil duty at the mercy of another. There may have been, and may be, persons who in their sanguine trust will not shrink from this result, and will console themselves with the notion that their loyalty and civil duty are to be committed to the custody of one much wiser than themselves. But I am sure that there are also "converts" who, when they perceive, will by word and act reject, the consequence which relentless logic draws for them. If, however, my proposition be true, there is no escape from the dilemma. Is it then true, or is it not true,

that Rome requires a convert, who now joins her, to
forfeit his moral and mental freedom, and to place
his loyalty and civil duty at the mercy of another?

In order to place this matter in as clear a light as
I can, it will be necessary to go back a little upon
our recent history.

A century ago we began to relax that system of
penal laws against Roman Catholics, at once petti-
fogging, base, and cruel, which Mr. Burke has
scathed and blasted with his immortal eloquence.

When this process had reached the point, at which
the question was whether they should be admitted
into Parliament, there arose a great and prolonged
national controversy; and some men, who at no
time of their lives were narrow-minded, such as Sir
Robert Peel, the Minister, resisted the concession.
The arguments in its favour were obvious and strong,
and they ultimately prevailed. But the strength of
the opposing party had lain in the allegation that,
from the nature and claims of the Papal power, it was
not possible for the consistent Roman Catholic to pay
to the crown of this country an entire allegiance, and
that the admission of persons, thus self-disabled, to
Parliament was inconsistent with the safety of the
State and nation; which had not very long before,
it may be observed, emerged from a struggle for
existence.

An answer to this argument was indispensable;
and it was supplied mainly from two sources. The

Josephine laws,* then still subsisting in the Austrian empire, and the arrangements which had been made after the peace of 1815 by Prussia and the German States with Pius VII. and Consalvi, proved that the Papal Court could submit to circumstances, and could allow material restraints even upon the exercise of its ecclesiastical prerogatives. Here, then, was a reply in the sense of the phrase *solvitur ambulando.* Much information of this class was collected for the information of Parliament and the country.† But there were also measures taken to learn, from the highest Roman Catholic authorities of this country, what was the exact situation of the members of that communion with respect to some of the better known exorbitancies of Papal assumption. Did the Pope claim any temporal jurisdiction? Did he still pretend to the exercise of a power to depose kings, release subjects from their allegiance, and incite them to revolt? Was faith to be kept with heretics? Did the Church still teach the doctrines of persecution? Now, to no

---

* See the work of Count dal Pozzo on the 'Austrian Ecclesiastical Law.' London: Murray, 1827. The Leopoldine Laws in Tuscany may also be mentioned.

† See ' Report from the Select Committee appointed to report the nature and substance of the Laws and Ordinances existing in Foreign. States, respecting the regulation of their Roman Catholic subjects in Ecclesiastical matters, and their intercourse with the See of Rome, or any other Foreign Ecclesiastical Jurisdiction.' Printed for the House of Commons in 1816 and 1817. Reprinted 1851.

one of these questions could the answer really be of the smallest immediate moment to this powerful and solidly compacted kingdom. They were topics selected by way of sample; and the intention was to elicit declarations showing generally that the fangs of the mediæval Popedom had been drawn, and its claws torn away; that the Roman system, however strict in its dogma, was perfectly compatible with civil liberty, and with the institutions of a free State moulded on a different religious basis from its own.

Answers in abundance were obtained, tending to show that the doctrines of deposition and persecution, of keeping no faith with heretics, and of universal dominion, were obsolete beyond revival; that every assurance could be given respecting them, except such as required the shame of a formal retractation; that they were in effect mere bugbears, unworthy to be taken into account by a nation, which prided itself on being made up of practical men.

But it was unquestionably felt that something more than the renunciation of these particular opinions was necessary in order to secure the full concession of civil rights to Roman Catholics. As to their individual loyalty, a State disposed to generous or candid interpretation had no reason to be uneasy. It was only with regard to requisitions, which might be made on them from another quarter, that apprehension could exist. It was reasonable that England

should desire to know not only what the Pope* might
do for himself, but to what demands, by the constitution of their Church, they were liable; and how far
it was possible that such demands could touch their
civil duty. The theory which placed every human
being, in things spiritual and things temporal, at the
feet of the Roman Pontiff, had not been an *idolum
specûs*, a mere theory of the chamber. Brain-power
never surpassed in the political history of the world
had been devoted for centuries to the single purpose
of working it into the practice of Christendom; had
in the West achieved for an impossible problem a
partial success; and had in the East punished the
obstinate independence of the Church by that Latin
conquest of Constantinople, which effectually prepared the way for the downfall of the Eastern empire;
and the establishment of the Turks in Europe. What
was really material therefore was, not whether the
Papal chair laid claim to this or that particular
power, but whether it laid claim to some power that
included them all, and whether that claim had
received such sanction from the authorities of the
Latin Church, that there remained within her borders

---

* At that period the eminent and able Bishop Doyle did not
scruple to write as follows : "We are taunted with the proceedings
of Popes. What, my Lord, have we Catholics to do with the
proceedings of Popes, or why should we be made accountable
for them?"—' Essay on the Catholic Claims.' To Lord Liver-
pool, 1826, p. 111.

absolutely no tenable standing-ground from which war
against it could be maintained. Did the Pope then
claim infallibility? Or did he, either without infallibility or with it (and if with it so much the worse),
claim an universal obedience from his flock? And
were these claims, either or both, affirmed in his
Church by authority which even the least Papal of
the members of that Church must admit to be binding upon conscience?

The two first of these questions were covered by
the third. And well it was that they were so covered.
For to them no satisfactory answer could even then
be given. The Popes had kept up, with comparatively little intermission, for well-nigh a thousand
years their claim to dogmatic infallibility; and had,
at periods within the same tract of time, often
enough made, and never retracted, that other claim
which is theoretically less but practically larger; their
claim to an obedience virtually universal from the
baptised members of the Church. To the third
question it was fortunately more practicable to pre-
scribe a satisfactory reply. It was well known that,
in the days of its glory and intellectual power, the
great Gallican Church had not only not admitted,
but had denied Papal infallibility, and had declared
that the local laws and usages of the Church could
not be set aside by the will of the Pontiff. Nay,
further, it was believed that in the main these had
been, down to the close of the last century, the pre-

vailing opinions of the Cisalpine Churches in communion with Rome. The Council of Constance had in act as well as word shown that the Pope's judgments, and the Pope himself, were triable by the assembled representatives of the Christian world. And the Council of Trent, notwithstanding the predominance in it of Italian and Roman influences, if it had not denied, yet had not affirmed either proposition.

All that remained was, to know what were the sentiments entertained on these vital points by the leaders and guides of Roman Catholic opinion nearest to our own doors. And here testimony was offered, which must not, and cannot, be forgotten. In part, this was the testimony of witnesses before the Committees of the two Houses in 1824 and 1825. I need quote two answers only, given by the Prelate, who more than any other represented his Church, and influenced the mind of this country in favour of concession at the time, namely, Bishop Doyle. He was asked,*

" In what, and how far, does the Roman Catholic profess to obey the Pope ? "

_____

* Committees of both Lords and Commons sat; the former in 1825, the latter in 1824-5. The References were identical, and ran as follows : " To inquire into the state of Ireland, more particularly with reference to the circumstances which may have led to disturbances in that part of the United Kingdom." Bishop Doyle was examined March 21, 1825, and April 21, 1825, before the Lords. The two citations in the text are taken from Bishop Doyle's evidence before the Commons' Committee, March 12, 1825, p. 190.

He replied :

" The Catholic professes to obey the Pope in matters which
regard his religious faith: and in those matters of ecclesiastical
discipline which have already been defined by the competent
authorities."

And again.

" Does that justify the objection that is made to Catholics, that
their allegiance is divided?"

" I do not think it does in any way. We are bound to obey
the Pope in those things that I have already mentioned. But
our obedience to the law, and the allegiance which we owe the
sovereign, are complete, and full, and perfect, and undivided,
inasmuch as they extend to all political, legal, and civil rights
of the king or of his subjects. I think the allegiance due to the
king, and the allegiance due to the Pope, are as distinct and as
divided in their nature, as any two things can possibly be."

Such is the opinion of the dead Prelate. We shall
presently hear the opinion of a living one. But the
sentiments of the dead man powerfully operated on
the open and trustful temper of this people to induce
them to grant, at the cost of so much popular feeling
and national tradition, the great and just concession
of 1829. That concession, without such declarations,
it would, to say the least, have been far more difficult
to obtain.

Now, bodies are usually held to be bound by the
evidence of their own selected and typical witnesses.
But in this instance the colleagues of those witnesses
thought fit also to speak collectively.

First let us quote from the collective " Declaration," in the year 1826, of the Vicars Apostolic, who,

with Episcopal authority, governed the Roman Catholics of Great Britain.

" The allegiance which Catholics hold to be due, and are bound to pay, to their Sovereign, and to the civil authority of the State, is perfect and undivided. . . . .
" They declare that neither the Pope, nor any other prelate or ecclesiastical person of the Roman Catholic Church . . . . has any right to interfere directly or indirectly in the Civil Government . . . . nor to oppose in any manner the performance of the civil duties which are due to the king."

Not less explicit was the Hierarchy of the Roman Communion in its " Pastoral Address to the Clergy and Laity of the Roman Catholic Church in Ireland," dated January 25, 1826. This address contains a Declaration, from which I extract the following words: —

" It is a duty which they owe to themselves, *as well as to their Protestant fellow-subjects*, whose good opinion they value, to endeavour once more to remove the false imputations that have been frequently cast upon the faith and discipline of that Church which is intrusted to their care, *that all may be enabled to know with accuracy their genuine principles.*"

In Article 11 :—

" They declare on oath their belief that it is not an article of the Catholic Faith, neither are they thereby required to believe, that the Pope is infallible."

and, after various recitals, they set forth

" After this full, explicit, and sworn declaration, we are utterly at a loss to conceive on what possible ground we could be justly charged with bearing towards our most gracious Sovereign only a divided allegiance."

Thus, besides much else that I will not stop to quote,

Papal infallibility was most solemnly declared to be
a matter on which each man might think as he
pleased; the Pope's power to claim obedience was
strictly and narrowly limited : it was expressly denied
that he had any title, direct or indirect, to interfere
in civil government. Of the right of the Pope to
define the limits which divide the civil from the
spiritual by his own authority, not one word is said
by the Prelates of either country.

Since that time, all these propositions have been
reversed. The Pope's infallibility, when he speaks
ex cathedrâ on faith and morals, has been declared,
with the assent of the Bishops of the Roman Church,
to be an article of faith, binding on the conscience of
every Christian; his claim to the obedience of his
spiritual subjects has been declared in like manner
without any practical limit or reserve; and his
supremacy, without any reserve of civil rights, has
been similarly affirmed to include everything which
relates to the discipline and government of the
Church throughout the world. And these doctrines,
we now know on the highest authority, it is of
necessity for salvation to believe.

Independently, however, of the Vatican Decrees
themselves, it is necessary for all who wish to under-
stand what has been the amount of the wonderful
change now consummated in the constitution of the
Latin Church, and what is the present degradation of
its Episcopal order, to observe also the change, amount-

ing to revolution, of form in the present, as compared with other conciliary decrees. Indeed, that spirit of centralisation, the excesses of which are as fatal to vigorous life in the Church as in the State, seems now nearly to have reached the last and furthest point of possible advancement and exaltation. When, in fact, we speak of the decrees of the Council of the Vatican, we use a phrase which will not bear strict examination. The Canons of the Council of Trent were, at least, the real Canons of a real Council : and the strain in which they are promulgated is this :—*Hæc sacrosancta, ecumenica, et generalis Tridentina Synodus, in Spiritu Sancto legitimè congregata, in eâ præsidentibus eisdem tribus apostolicis Legatis, hortatur,* or *docet,* or *statuit,* or *decernit* (*b*), and the like : and its canons, as published in Rome, are " *Canones et decreta Sacrosancti ecumenici Concilii Tridentini* " (*c*),* and so forth. But what we have now to do with is the *Constitutio Dogmatica Prima de Ecclesiâ Christi, edita in Sessione tertiâ* of the Vatican Council. It is not a constitution made by the Council, but one promulgated in the Council.† And who is it that legislates and decrees? It is *Pius Episcopus,*

_____

(*b*) (*c*) For translations of these passages, see p. 71.

* ' Romæ : in Collegio urbano de Propagandâ Fide.' 1833.

† I am aware that, as some hold, this was the case with the Council of the Lateran in A.D. 1215. But, first, this has not been established : secondly, the very gist of the evil we are dealing with consists in following (and enforcing) precedents from the age of Pope Innocent III.

servus servorum Dei (*d*): and the seductive plural of his *docemus et declaramus* is simply the dignified and ceremonious " We " of Royal declarations. The document is dated *Pontificatûs nostri Anno XXV:* and the humble share of the assembled Episcopate in the transaction is represented by *sacro approbante concilio.* And now for the propositions themselves.

First comes the Pope's infallibility :—

"Docemus, et divinitus revelatum dogma esse definimus, Romanum Pontificem, cum ex Cathedrâ loquitur, id est cum, omnium Christianorum Pastoris et Doctoris munere fungens, pro supremâ suâ Apostolicâ auctoritate doctrinam de fide vel moribus ab universâ Ecclesiâ tenendam definit, per assistentiam divinam, ipsi in Beato Petro promissam, eâ infallibilitate pollere, quâ Divinus Redemptor Ecclesiam suam in definiendâ doctrinâ de fide vel moribus instructam esse voluit : ideoque ejus Romani Pontificis definitiones ex sese non antem ex consensu Ecclesiæ irreformabiles esse " (*e*).*

Will it, then, be said that the infallibility of the Pope accrues only when he speaks *ex cathedrâ* ? No doubt this is a very material consideration for those who have been told that the private conscience is to derive comfort and assurance from the emanations of the Papal Chair : for there is no established or accepted definition of the phrase *ex cathedrâ*, and he has no power to obtain one, and no guide to direct him in his choice among some twelve theories on the subject, which, it is said, are bandied to and fro

---

(*d*) (*e*) For translations of these passages, see p. 71.

* 'Constitutio de Ecclesiâ,' c. iv.

among Roman theologians, except the despised and
discarded agency of his private judgment. But while
thus sorely tantalised, he is not one whit protected.
For there is still one person, and one only, who can
unquestionably declare *ex cathedrâ* what is *ex cathedrâ*
and what is not, and who can declare it when and as
he pleases. That person is the Pope himself. The
provision is, that no document he issues shall be valid
without a seal : but the seal remains under his own
sole lock and key.

Again, it may be sought to plead, that the Pope
is, after all, only operating by sanctions which unquestionably belong to the religious domain. He .
does not propose to invade the country, to seize
Woolwich, or burn Portsmouth. He will only, at
the worst, excommunicate opponents, as he has ex-
communicated Dr. von Döllinger and others. Is this
a good answer? After all, even in the Middle Ages,
it was not by the direct action of fleets and armies of
their own that the Popes contended with kings who
were refractory ; it was mainly by interdicts, and by
the refusal, which they entailed when the Bishops
were not brave enough to refuse their publication,
of religious offices to the people. It was thus that
England suffered under John, France under Philip
Augustus, Leon under Alphonso the Noble, and
every country in its turn. But the inference may be
drawn that they who, while using spiritual weapons
for such an end, do not employ temporal means, only

fail to employ them because they have them not.
A religious society, which delivers volleys of spiritual
censures in order to impede the performance of
civil duties, does all the mischief that is in its power
to do, and brings into question, in the face of the
State, its title to civil protection.

Will it be said, finally, that the Infallibility touches
only matter of faith and morals? Only matter of
morals! Will any of the Roman casuists kindly
acquaint us what are the departments and functions
of human life which do not and cannot fall within the
domain of morals? If they will not tell us, we must
look elsewhere. In his work entitled 'Literature
and Dogma,' * Mr. Matthew Arnold quaintly informs
us—as they tell us nowadays how many parts of our
poor bodies are solid, and how many aqueous—that
about seventy-five per cent. of all we do belongs to
the department of " conduct." Conduct and morals,
we may suppose, are nearly co-extensive. Three-
fourths, then, of life are thus handed over. But who
will guarantee to us the other fourth? Certainly
not St. Paul; who says, " Whether therefore ye eat,
or drink, or whatsoever ye do, do *all* to the glory of
God." And " Whatsoever ye do, in word or in
deed, do *all* in the name of the Lord Jesus." † No!
Such a distinction would be the unworthy device of a
shallow policy, vainly used to hide the daring of that

---

* Pages 15, 44. 　　　 † 1 Cor. x. 31 ; Col. iii. 7.

wild ambition which at Rome, not from the throne but from behind the throne, prompts the movements of the Vatican. I care not to ask if there be dregs or tatters of human life, such as can escape from the description and boundary of morals. I submit that Duty is a power which rises with us in the morning, and goes to rest with us at night. It is co-extensive with the action of our intelligence. It is the shadow which cleaves to us go where we will, and which only leaves us when we leave the light of life. So then it is the supreme direction of us in respect to all Duty, which the Pontiff declares to belong to him, *sacro approbante concilio*: and this declaration he makes, not as an otiose opinion of the schools, but *cunctis fidelibus credendam et tenendam* (*f*).

But we shall now see that, even if a loophole had at this point been left unclosed, the void is supplied by another provision of the Decrees. While the reach of the Infallibility is as wide as it may please the Pope, or those who may prompt the Pope, to make it, there is something wider still, and that is the claim to an absolute and entire Obedience. This Obedience is to be rendered to his orders in the cases I shall proceed to point out, without any qualifying condition, such as the *ex cathedrâ*. The sounding name of Infallibility has so fascinated the public mind, and riveted it on the Fourth Chapter of the

---

(*f*) For translation of this passage, see p. 72.

Constitution *de Ecclesiâ*, that its near neighbour, the
Third Chapter, has, at least in my opinion, received
very much less than justice.   Let us turn to it.

"Cujuscunque ritûs et dignitatis pastores atque fideles, tam
seorsum singuli quam simul omnes, officio hierarchicæ subordi-
nationis veræque obedientiæ obstringuntur, non solum in rebus,
quæ ad fidem et mores, sed etiam in iis, quæ ad disciplinam et
regimen Ecclesiæ per totum orbem diffusæ pertinent. . . . . Hæc
est Catholicæ veritatis doctrina, a quâ deviare, salvâ fide atque
salute, nemo potest (*g*). . . . .

"Docemus etiam et declaramus eum esse judicem supremum
fidelium, et in omnibus causis ad examen ecclesiasticum spec-
tantibus ad ipsius posse judicium recurri : Sedis vero Apostolicæ,
cujus auctoritate major non est, judicium a nemine fore retrac-
tandum. Neque cuiquam de ejus licere judicare judicio."[*]

Even, therefore, where the judgments of the Pope
do not present the credentials of infallibility, they
are unappealable and irreversible : no person may pass
judgment upon them ; and all men, clerical and lay,
dispersedly or in the aggregate, are bound truly to
obey them ; and from this rule of Catholic truth no
man can depart, save at the peril of his salvation.
Surely, it is allowable to say that this Third Chapter
on universal obedience is a formidable rival to the
Fourth Chapter on Infallibility.   Indeed, to an ob-
server from without, it seems to leave the dignity to
the other, but to reserve the stringency and efficiency
to itself.   The Fourth Chapter is the Merovingian
Monarch ; the Third is the Carolingian Mayor of the

(*g*) For translations of these passages, see p. 72.

[*] 'Dogmatic Constitutions,' &c., c. iii. : Dublin, 1870, pp. 30-32.

Palace. The Fourth has an overawing splendour; the Third, an iron gripe. Little does it matter to me whether my superior claims infallibility, so long as he is entitled to demand and exact conformity. This, it will be observed, he demands even in cases not covered by his infallibility; cases, therefore, in which he admits it to be possible that he may be wrong, but finds it intolerable to be told so. As he must be obeyed in all his judgments though not *ex cathedrâ*, it seems a pity he could not likewise give the comforting assurance that, they are all certain to be right.

But why this ostensible reduplication, this apparent surplusage? Why did the astute contrivers of this tangled scheme conclude that they could not afford to rest content with pledging the Council to Infallibility in terms which are not only wide to a high degree, but elastic beyond all measure?

Though they must have known perfectly well that " faith and morals " carried everything, or everything worth having, in the purely individual sphere, they also knew just as well that, even where the individual was subjugated, they might and would still have to deal with the State.

In mediæval history, this distinction is not only clear, but glaring. Outside the borders of some narrow and proscribed sect, now and then emerging, we never, or scarcely ever, hear of private and personal resistance to the Pope. The manful " Protestantism " of mediæval times had its activity almost

entirely in the sphere of public, national, and state
rights. Too much attention, in my opinion, cannot
be fastened on this point. It is the very root and
kernel of the matter. Individual servitude, however
abject, will not satisfy the party now dominant in
the Latin Church : the State must also be a slave.

Our Saviour had recognised as distinct the two
provinces of the civil rule and the Church : had no-
where intimated that the spiritual authority was to
claim the disposal of physical force, and to control in
its own domain the authority which is alone responsible
for external peace, order, and safety among civilised
communities of men. It has been alike the peculiarity, the pride, and the misfortune of the Roman
Church, among Christian communities, to allow to
itself an unbounded use, as far as its power would go,
of earthly instruments for spiritual ends. We have
seen with what ample assurances* this nation and
Parliament were fed in 1826 ; how well and roundly
the full and undivided rights of the civil power, and
the separation of the two jurisdictions, were affirmed.
All this had at length been undone, as far as Popes
could undo it, in the Syllabus and the Encyclical. It
remained to complete the undoing, through the sub-
serviency or pliability of the Council.

And the work is now truly complete. Lest it
should be said that supremacy in faith and morals, full

* See further, Appendix B.

dominion over personal belief and conduct, did not
cover the collective action of men in States, a third
province was opened, not indeed to the abstract assertion of Infallibility, but to the far more practical and
decisive demand of absolute Obedience. And this
is the proper work of the Third Chapter, to which I
am endeavouring to do a tardy justice. Let us listen
again to its few but pregnant words on the point :

"Non solum in rebus, quæ ad fidem et mores, sed etiam in
iis, quæ ad disciplinam et regimen Ecclesiæ per totum orbem
diffusæ pertinent" (h).

Absolute obedience, it is boldly declared, is due to
the Pope, at the peril of salvation, not alone in faith,
in morals, but in all things which concern the discipline and government of the Church. Thus are swept
into the Papal net whole multitudes of facts, whole
systems of government, prevailing, though in different degrees, in every country of the world. Even
in the United States, where the severance between
Church and State is supposed to be complete, a long
catalogue might be drawn of subjects belonging to
the domain and competency of the State, but also
undeniably affecting the government of the Church ;
such as, by way of example, marriage, burial, education, prison discipline, blasphemy, poor-relief, in-
corporation, mortmain, religious endowments, vows
of celibacy and obedience. In Europe the circle is

(h) For translation of this passage, see p. 72.

far wider, the points of contact and of interlacing
almost innumerable.   But on all matters, respecting
which any Pope may think proper to declare that they
concern either faith, or morals, or the government
or discipline of the Church, he claims, with the
approval of a Council undoubtedly Ecumenical in
the Roman sense, the absolute obedience, at the peril
of salvation, of every member of his communion.

It seems not as yet to have been thought wise to
pledge the Council in terms to the Syllabus and the
Encyclical.   That achievement is probably reserved
for some one of its sittings yet to come.   In the
meantime it is well to remember, that this claim in
respect of all things affecting the discipline and
government of the Church, as well as faith and
conduct, is lodged in open day by and in the reign
of a Pontiff, who has condemned free speech, free
writing, a free press, toleration of nonconformity,
liberty of conscience, the study of civil and philosophical matters in independence of the ecclesiastical
authority, marriage unless sacramentally contracted,
and the definition by the State of the civil rights
(*jura*) of the Church ; who has demanded for the
Church, therefore, the title to define its own civil
rights, together with a divine right to civil im-
munities, and a right to use physical force ; and who
has also proudly asserted that the Popes of the Middle
Ages with their councils did not invade the rights of
princes: as for example, Gregory VII., of the Emperor

Henry IV.; Innocent III., of Raymond of Toulouse; Paul III., in deposing Henry VIII.; or Pius V., in performing the like paternal office for Elizabeth.

I submit, then, that my fourth proposition is true: and that England is entitled to ask, and to know, in what way the obedience required by the Pope and the Council of the Vatican is to be reconciled with the integrity of civil allegiance?

It has been shown that the Head of their Church, so supported as undoubtedly to speak with its highest authority, claims from Roman Catholics a plenary obedience to whatever he may desire in relation not to faith but to morals, and not only to these, but to all that concerns the government and discipline of the Church : that, of this, much lies within the domain of the State : that, to obviate all misapprehension, the Pope demands for himself the right to determine the province of his own rights, and has so defined it in formal documents, as to warrant any and every invasion of the civil sphere ; and that this new version of the principles of the Papal Church inexorably binds its members to the admission of these exorbitant claims, without any refuge or reservation on behalf of their duty to the Crown.

Under circumstances such as these, it seems not too much to ask of them to confirm the opinion which we, as fellow-countrymen, entertain of them, by sweeping away, in such manner and terms as they may think best, the presumptive imputations which their ecclesiastical rulers at Rome, acting autocratically, appear to have brought upon their capacity to pay a solid and undivided allegiance; and to fulfil the engagement which their Bishops, as political sponsors, promised and declared for them in 1825.

It would be impertinent, as well as needless, to suggest what should be said. All that is requisite is to indicate in substance that which (if the foregoing argument be sound) is not wanted, and that which is. What is not wanted is vague and general assertion, of whatever kind, and however sincere. What is wanted, and that in the most specific form and the clearest terms, I take to be one of two things; that is to say, either—

I. A demonstration that neither in the name of faith, nor in the name of morals, nor in the name of the government or discipline of the Church, is the Pope of Rome able, by virtue of the powers asserted for him by the Vatican decree, to make any claim upon those who adhere to his communion, of such a nature as can impair the integrity of their civil allegiance; or else,

II. That, if and when such claim is made, it will even although resting on the definitions of the Vatican, be repelled and rejected; just as Bishop Doyle, when he was asked what the Roman Catholic clergy would do if the Pope intermeddled with their religion, replied frankly, " The consequence would be, that we should oppose him by every means in our power, even by the exercise of our spiritual authority." *

In the absence of explicit 'assurances to this effect, we should appear to be led, nay, driven, by just reasoning upon that documentary evidence, to the conclusions:—

1. That the Pope, authorised by his Council, claims for himself the domain (*a*) of faith, (*b*) of morals, (*c*) of all that concerns the government and discipline of the Church.

2. That he in like manner claims the power of determining the limits of those domains.

3. That he does not sever them, by any acknowledged or intelligible line, from the domains of civil duty and allegiance.

4. That he therefore claims, and claims from the month of July 1870 onwards with plenary authority, from every convert and member of his Church, that he shall "place his loyalty and civil duty at the mercy of another:" that other being himself.

V. Being True, are the Propositions Material?

But next, if these propositions be true, are they also material? The claims cannot, as I much fear, be denied to have been made. It cannot be denied that the Bishops, who govern in things spiritual more

---

* 'Report,' March 18, 1826, p. 191.

than five millions (or nearly one-sixth) of the inhabitants of the United Kingdom, have in some cases promoted, in all cases accepted, these claims. It has been a favourite purpose of my life not to conjure up, but to conjure down, public alarms. I am not now going to pretend that either foreign foe or domestic treason can, at the bidding of the Court of Rome, disturb these peaceful shores. But though such fears may be visionary, it is more visionary still to suppose for one moment that the claims of Gregory VII., of Innocent III., and of Boniface VIII., have been disinterred, in the nineteenth century, like hideous mummies picked out of Egyptian sarcophagi, in the interests of archæology, or without a definite and practical aim. As rational beings, we must rest assured that only with a very clearly conceived and foregone purpose have these astonishing reassertions been paraded before the world. What is that purpose?

I can well believe that it is in part theological. There have always been, and there still are, no small proportion of our race, and those by no means in all respects the worst, who are sorely open to the temptation, especially in times of religious disturbance, to discharge their spiritual responsibilities by *power of attorney*. As advertising Houses find custom in proportion, not so much to the solidity of their resources as to the magniloquence of their promises and assurances, so theological boldness in the extension of such claims is sure to pay, by widening certain circles of devoted adherents, however it may repel the mass of mankind. There were two special encouragements to this enterprise at the present day : one of them the perhaps unconscious but manifest leaning of some, outside the Roman precinct, to undue exaltation of Church power; the other the reaction, which is and must be brought about in favour of superstition, by the levity of the destructive speculations so widely current, and the notable hardihood of the anti-Christian writing of the day.

But it is impossible to account sufficiently in this manner for the particular course which has been actually pursued by the Roman Court. All morbid spiritual appetites would have been amply satisfied by claims to infallibility in creed, to the prerogative of miracle, to dominion over the unseen world. In truth there was occasion, in this view, for nothing, except a liberal supply of Salmonean thunder :—

" Dum flammas Jovis, et sonitus imitatur Olympi."*

All this could have been managed by a few Tetzels, judiciously distributed over Europe. Therefore the question still remains, Why did that Court, with policy for ever in its eye, lodge such formidable demands for power of the vulgar kind in that sphere which is visible, and where hard knocks can undoubtedly be given as well as received ?

* Æn. vi. 586.

It must be for some political object, of a very
tangible kind, that the risks of so daring a raid upon
the civil sphere have been deliberately run.

A daring raid it is. For it is most evident that the
very assertion of principles which establish an ex-
emption from allegiance, or which impair its com-
pleteness, goes, in many other countries of Europe,
far more directly than with us, to the creation of political strife, and to dangers of the most material and
tangible kind. The struggle, now proceeding in
Germany, at once occurs to the mind as a palmary
instance. I am not competent to give any opinion
upon the particulars of that struggle. The institutions of Germany, and the relative estimate of State
power and individual freedom, are materially different
from ours. But I must say as much as this. First,
it is not Prussia alone · that is touched; elsewhere,
too, the bone lies ready, though the contention may
be delayed. In other States, in Austria particularly,
there are recent laws in force, raising much the same
issues as the Falck laws have raised. But the
Roman Court possesses in perfection one art, the art
of waiting; and it is her wise maxim to fight but
one enemy at a time. Secondly, if I have truly
represented the claims promulgated from the Vatican, it is difficult to deny that those claims, and the
power which has made them, are primarily responsible for the pains and perils, whatever they may be,
of the present conflict between German and Roman

enactments. And that which was once truly said of
France, may now also be said with not less truth
of Germany : when Germany is disquieted, Europe
cannot be at rest.

I should feel less anxiety on this subject had the
Supreme Pontiff frankly recognised his altered position since the events of 1870 ; and, in language as
clear, if not as emphatic, as that in which he has
proscribed modern civilisation, given to Europe the
assurance that he would be no party to the re-
establishment by blood and violence of the Temporal Power of the Church. It is easy to conceive
that his personal benevolence, no less than his
feelings as an Italian, must have inclined him individually towards a course so humane ; and I should
add, if I might do it without presumption, so pru-
dent. With what appears to an English eye a
lavish prodigality, successive Italian Governments
have made over the ecclesiastical powers and privi-
leges of the Monarchy, not to the Church of the
country for the revival of the ancient, popular, and
self-governing elements of its constitution, but to the
Papal Chair, for the establishment of ecclesiastical
despotism, and the suppression of the last vestiges of
independence. This course, so difficult for a foreigner
to appreciate, or even to justify, has been met, not by
reciprocal conciliation, but by a constant fire of
denunciations and complaints. When the tone
of these denunciations and complaints is compared

E

with the language of the authorised and favoured
Papal organs in the press, and of the Ultramontane
party (now the sole legitimate party of the Latin
Church) throughout Europe, it leads many to the
painful and revolting conclusion that there is a fixed
purpose among the secret inspirers of Roman policy
to pursue, by the road of force, upon the arrival of
any favourable opportunity, the favourite project
of re-erecting the terrestrial throne of the Popedom,
even if it can only be re-erected on the ashes of the
city, and amidst the whitening bones of the people.*

It is difficult to conceive or contemplate the effects of
such an endeavour.   But the existence at this day
of the policy, even in bare idea, is itself a portentous
evil. · I do not hesitate to say that it is an incentive
to general disturbance, a premium upon European
wars.   It is in my opinion not sanguine only, but
almost ridiculous to imagine that such a project could
eventually succeed ; but it is difficult to over-estimate
the effect which it might produce in generating and
exasperating strife.   It might even, to some extent,
disturb and paralyse the action of such Governments
as might interpose for no separate purpose of their
own, but only with a view to the maintenance or
restoration of the general peace.   If the baleful
Power which is expressed by the phrase *Curia
Romana*, and not at all adequately rendered in its

---

* Appendix C.

historic force by the usual English equivalent
"Court of Rome," really entertains the scheme, it
doubtless counts on the support in every country of
an organised and devoted party; which, when it can
command the scales of political power, will promote
interference, and, when it is in a minority, will work
for securing neutrality. As the peace of Europe
may be in jeopardy, and as the duties even of England, as one (so to speak) of its constabulary authorities, might come to be in question, it would be most
interesting to know the mental attitude of our Roman
Catholic fellow-countrymen in England and Ireland
with reference to the subject; and it seems to be one,
on which we are entitled to solicit information.

For there cannot be the smallest doubt that the
temporal power of the Popedom comes within the
true meaning of the words used at the Vatican to
describe the subjects on which the Pope is authorised
to claim, under awful sanctions, the obedience of the
"faithful." It is even possible that we have here
the key to the enlargement of the province of
Obedience beyond the limits of Infallibility, and to
the introduction of the remarkable phrase *ad disciplinam et regimen Ecclesiæ*. No impartial person can
deny that the question of the temporal power very
evidently concerns the discipline and government of
the Church—concerns it, and most mischievously as
I should venture to think; but in the opinion, up to
a late date, of many Roman Catholics, not only most

beneficially, but even essentially. Let it be remembered, that such a man as the late Count Montalembert, who in his general politics was of the Liberal party, did not scruple to hold that the millions of Roman Catholics throughout the world were co-partners with the inhabitants of the States of the Church in regard to their civil government; and, as constituting the vast majority, were of course entitled to override them. It was also rather commonly held, a quarter of a century ago, that the question of the States of the Church was one with which none but Roman Catholic Powers could have anything to do. This doctrine, I must own, was to me at all times unintelligible. It is now, to say the least, hopelessly and irrecoverably obsolete.

Archbishop Manning, who is the head of the Papal Church in England, and whose ecclesiastical tone is supposed to be in the closest accordance with that of his headquarters, has not thought it too much to say that the civil order of all Christendom is the offspring of the Temporal Power, and has the Temporal Power for its keystone; that on the destruction of the Temporal Power "the laws of nations would at once fall in ruins;" that (our old friend) the deposing Power "taught subjects obedience and princes clemency."* Nay, this high

---

* 'Three Lectures on the Temporal Sovereignty of the Popes,' 1860, pp. 34, 46, 47, 58 9, 63.

authority has proceeded further; and has elevated the Temporal Power to the rank of necessary doctrine.

" The Catholic Church cannot be silent, it cannot hold its peace; it cannot cease to preach the doctrines of Revelation, not only of the Trinity and of the Incarnation, but likewise of the Seven Sacraments, and of the Infallibility of the Church of God, and of the necessity of Unity, and of the Sovereignty, both spiritual and temporal, of the Holy See." *

I never, for my own part, heard that the work containing this remarkable passage was placed in the ' Index Prohibitorum Librorum.' On the contrary, its distinguished author was elevated, on the first opportunity, to the headship of the Roman Episcopacy in England, and to the guidance of the million or thereabouts of souls in its communion. And the more recent utterances of the oracle have not descended from the high level of those already cited. They have, indeed, the recommendation of a comment, not without fair claims to authority, on the recent declarations of the Pope and the Council; and of one which goes to prove how far I am from having exaggerated or strained in the foregoing pages the meaning of those declarations. Especially does this hold good on the one point, the most vital of the whole— the title to define the border line of the two provinces, which the Archbishop not unfairly takes to be the true

* ' The present Crisis of the Holy See.' By H. E. Manning, D.D. London, 1861, p. 73.

criterion of supremacy, as between rival powers like the Church and the State.

" If, then, the civil power be not competent to decide the limits of the spiritual power, and if the spiritual power can define, with a divine certainty, its own limits, it is evidently supreme. Or, in other words, the spiritual power knows, with divine certainty, the limits of its own jurisdiction : and it knows therefore the limits and the competence of the civil power. It is thereby, in matters of religion and conscience, supreme. I do not see how this can be denied without denying Christianity. And if this be so, this is the doctrine of the Bull *Unam Sanctam*,* and of the Syllabus, and of the Vatican Council. It is, in fact, Ultramontanism, for this term means neither less nor more. The Church, therefore, is separate and supreme.

" Let us then ascertain somewhat further, what is the meaning of supreme. Any power which is independent, *and can alone fix the limits of its own jurisdiction, and can thereby fix the limits of all other jurisdictions, is*, ipso facto, *supreme*.† But the Church of Jesus Christ, within the sphere of revelation, of faith and morals, is all this, or is nothing, or worse than nothing, an imposture and an usurpation—that is, it is Christ or Antichrist." ‡

But the whole pamphlet should be read by those who desire to know the true sense of the Papal declarations and Vatican decrees, as they are understood by the most favoured ecclesiastics; understood, I am bound to own, so far as I can see, in their natural, legitimate, and inevitable sense. Such readers will

---

* On the Bull *Unam Sanctam*, "of a most odious kind ;" see Bishop Doyle's Essay, already cited. He thus describes it.

† The italics are not in the original.

‡ 'Cæsarism and Ultramontanism.' By Archbishop Manning, 1874, pp. 35-6.

be assisted by the treatise in seeing clearly, and in
admitting frankly that, whatever demands may hereafter, and in whatever circumstances, be made upon
us, we shall be unable to advance with any fairness
the plea that it has been done without due notice.

There are millions upon millions of the Protestants
of this country, who would agree with Archbishop
Manning, if he were simply telling us that Divine
truth is not to be sought from the lips of the State,
nor to be sacrificed at its command. But those
millions would tell him, in return, that the State, as
the power which is alone responsible for the external
order of the world, can alone conclusively and finally
be competent to determine what is to take place in
the sphere of that external order.

I have shown, then, that the Propositions, especially that which has been felt to be the chief one
among them, being true, are also material; material
to be generally known, and clearly understood, and
well considered, on civil grounds; inasmuch as they
invade, at a multitude of points, the civil sphere, and
seem even to have no very remote or shadowy connection with the future peace and security of Christendom.

VI. Were the Propositions proper to be set forth by the present Writer?

There remains yet before us only the shortest and
least significant portion of the inquiry, namely,

whether these things, being true, and being material
to be said, were also proper to be said by me. I must
ask pardon, if a tone of egotism be detected in this
necessarily subordinate portion of my remarks.

For thirty years, and in a great variety of circumstances, in office and as an independent Member of
Parliament, in majorities and in small minorities, and
during the larger portion of the time * as the repre-
sentative of a great constituency, mainly clerical, I
have, with others, laboured to maintain and extend
the civil rights of my Roman Catholic fellow-countrymen. The Liberal party of this country, with which
I have been commonly associated, has suffered, and
sometimes suffered heavily, in public favour and in
influence, from the belief that it was too ardent in the
pursuit of that policy ; while at the same time it has
always been in the worst odour with the Court of
Rome, in consequence of its (I hope) unalterable
attachment to Italian liberty and independence. I
have sometimes been the spokesman of that party in
recommendations which have tended to foster in fact
the imputation I have mentioned, though not to
warrant it as matter of reason. But it has existed in
fact. So that while (as I think) general justice to
society required that these things which I have now
set forth should be written, special justice, as towards
the party to which I am loyally attached, and which

---

* From 1847 to 1865 I sat for the University of Oxford.

I may have had a share in thus placing at a disadvantage before our countrymen, made it, to say the least, becoming that I should not shrink from writing them.

In discharging that office, I have sought to perform the part not of a theological partisan, but simply of a good citizen ; of one hopeful that many of his Roman Catholic friends and fellow-countrymen, who are, to say the least of it, as good citizens as himself, may perceive that the case is not a frivolous case, but one that merits their attention.

I will next proceed to give the reason why, up to a recent date, I have thought it right in the main to leave to any others, who might feel it, the duty of dealing in detail with this question.

The great change, which seems to me to have been brought about in the position of Roman Catholic Christians as citizens, reached its consummation, and came into full operation in July 1870, by the proceedings or so-called decrees of the Vatican Council.

Up to that time, opinion in the Roman Church on all matters involving civil liberty, though partially and sometimes widely intimidated, was free wherever it was resolute. During the Middle Ages, heresy was often extinguished in blood, but in every Cisalpine country a principle of liberty, to a great extent, held its own, and national life refused to be put down. Nay more, these precious and inestimable gifts had not infrequently for their champions a local prelacy and clergy. The Constitutions of Clarendon, cursed

from the Papal throne, had the support of the
English Bishops. Stephen Langton, appointed directly, through an extraordinary stretch of power,
by Innocent III., to the See of Canterbury, headed
the Barons of England in extorting from the Papal
minion John, the worst and basest of all our
Sovereigns, that Magna Charta, which the Pope
at once visited with his anathemas. In the reign
of Henry VIII., it was Tunstal, Bishop of Durham,
who first wrote against the Papal domination.
Tunstal was followed by Gardiner; and even the
recognition of the Royal Headship was voted by
the clergy, not under Cranmer, but under his unsus-
pected predecessor Warham. Strong and domineer-
ing as was the high Papal party in those centuries,
the resistance was manful. Thrice in history, it
seemed as if what we may call the Constitutional
party in the Church was about to triumph : first, at
the epoch of the Council of Constance ; secondly,
when the French Episcopate was in conflict with
Pope Innocent XI. ; thirdly, when Clement XIV.
levelled with the dust the deadliest foes that mental
and moral liberty have ever known. But from July
1870, this state of things has passed away, and the
death-warrant of that Constitutional party has been
signed, and sealed, and promulgated in form.

Before that time arrived, although I had used expressions sufficiently indicative as to the tendency of
things in the great Latin Communion, yet I had for

very many years felt it to be the first and para-
mount duty of the British Legislature, whatever
Rome might say or do, to give to Ireland all that
justice could demand, in regard to matters of conscience and of civil equality, and thus to set herself
right in the opinion of the civilised world. So far
from seeing, what some believed they saw, a spirit of
unworthy compliance in such a course, it appeared
to me the only one which suited either the dignity
or the duty of my country. While this debt remained
unpaid, both before and after 1870, I did not think
it my province to open formally a line of argument
on a question of prospective rather than immediate
moment, which might have prejudiced the matter of
duty lying nearest our hand, and morally injured
Great Britain not less than Ireland, Churchmen and
Nonconformists not less than adherents of the Papal
Communion, by slackening the disposition to pay the
debt of justice. When Parliament had passed the
Church Act of 1869 and the Land Act of 1870, there
remained only, under the great head of Imperial
equity, one serious question to be dealt with—that of
the higher Education. I consider that the Liberal majority in the House of Commons, and the Government
to which I had the honour and satisfaction to belong,
formally tendered payment in full of this portion of
the debt by the Irish University Bill of February
1873. Some indeed think, that it was overpaid: a
question into which this is manifestly not the place to

enter. But the Roman Catholic prelacy of Ireland thought fit to procure the rejection of that measure, by the direct influence which they exercised over a certain number of Irish Members of Parliament, and by the temptation which they thus offered—the bid, in effect, which (to use a homely phrase) they made, to attract the support of the Tory Opposition. Their efforts were crowned with a complete success. From that time forward I have felt that the situation was changed, and that important matters would have to be cleared by suitable explanations. The debt to Ireland had been paid : a debt to the country at large had still to be disposed of, and this has come to be the duty of the hour. So long, indeed, as I continued to be Prime Minister, I should not have considered a broad political discussion on a general question suitable to proceed from me ; while neither I nor (I am certain) my colleagues would have been disposed to run the risk of stirring popular passions by a vulgar and unexplained appeal. But every difficulty, arising from the necessary limitations of an official position, has now been removed.

VII. On the Home Policy of the Future.

I could not, however, conclude these observations without anticipating and answering an inquiry they suggest. "Are they, then," it will be asked, "a recantation and a regret ; and what are they meant

to recommend as the policy of the future?" My
reply shall be succinct and plain. Of what the
Liberal party has accomplished, by word or deed, in
establishing the full civil equality of Roman Catholics, I regret nothing, and I recant nothing.

It is certainly a political misfortune that, during
the last thirty years, a Church so tainted in its views
of civil obedience, and so unduly capable of changing
its front and language after Emancipation from what
it had been before, like an actor who has to perform
several characters in one piece, should have acquired an
extension of its hold upon the highest classes of this
country. The conquests have been chiefly, as might
have been expected, among women; but the number
of male converts, or captives (as I might prefer to
call them), has not been inconsiderable. There is no
doubt, that every one of these secessions is in the
nature of a considerable moral and social severance.
The breadth of this gap varies, according to varieties
of individual character. But it is too commonly a
wide one. Too commonly, the spirit of the neophyte is
expressed by the words which have become notorious :
" a Catholic first, an Englishman afterwards." Words
which properly convey no more than a truism ; for
every Christian must seek to place his religion even
before his country in his inner heart. But very far
from a truism in the sense in which we have been led
to construe them. We take them to mean that the
" convert " intends, in case of any conflict between

the Queen and the Pope, to follow the Pope, and
let the Queen shift for herself; which, happily, she
can well do.

Usually, in this country, a movement in the highest
class would raise a presumption of a similar movement in the mass. It is not so here. Rumours have
gone about that the proportion of members of the
Papal Church to the population has increased, especially in England. But these rumours would seem
to be confuted by authentic figures. The Roman
Catholic Marriages, which supply a competent test,
and which were 4·89 per cent. of the whole in 1854,
and 4·62 per cent. in 1859, were 4·09 per cent. in
1869, and 4·02 per cent. in 1871.

There is something at the least abnormal in such
a partial growth, taking effect as it does among the
wealthy and noble, while the people cannot be
charmed, by any incantation, into the Roman camp.
The original Gospel was supposed to be meant especially for the poor; but the gospel of the nineteenth
century from Rome courts another and less modest
destination. If the Pope does not control more
souls among us, he certainly controls more acres.

The severance, however, of a certain number of
lords of the soil from those who till it, can be borne.
And so I trust will in like manner be endured the
new and very real " aggression " of the principles promulgated by Papal authority, whether they are or
are not loyally disclaimed. In this matter, each man

is his own judge and his own guide : I can speak for
myself. I am no longer able to say, as I would have
said before 1870, " There is nothing in the necessary
belief of the Roman Catholic which can appear to
impeach his full civil title; for, whatsoever be the
follies of ecclesiastical power in his Church, his
Church itself has not required of him, with binding
authority, to assent to any principles inconsistent
with his civil duty." That ground is now, for the
present at least, cut from under my feet. What
then is to be our course of policy hereafter ? First
let me say that, as regards the great Imperial
settlement, achieved by slow degrees, which has
admitted men of all creeds subsisting among us to
Parliament, that I conceive to be so determined
beyond all doubt or question, as to have become one
of the deep foundation-stones of the existing Constitution. But inasmuch as, short of this great charter of
public liberty, and independently of all that has been
done, there are pending matters of comparatively
minor moment which have been, or may be, subjects
of discussion, not without interest attaching to them,
I can suppose a question to arise in the minds of
some. My own views and intentions in the future
are of the smallest significance. But, if the arguments I have here offered make it my duty to declare
them, I say at once the future will be exactly as the
past : in the little that depends on me, I shall be
guided hereafter, as heretofore, by the rule of main-

taining equal civil rights irrespectively of religious differences; and shall resist all attempts to exclude the members of the Roman Church from the benefit of that rule. Indeed I may say that I have already given conclusive indications of this view, by supporting in Parliament, as a Minister, since 1870, the repeal of the Ecclesiastical Titles Act, for what I think ample reasons. Not only because the time has not yet come when we can assume the consequences of the revolutionary measures of 1870 to have been thoroughly weighed and digested by all capable men in the Roman Communion. Not only because so great a numerical proportion are, as I have before observed, necessarily incapable of mastering, and forming their personal judgment upon, the case. Quite irrespectively even of these considerations, I hold that our onward even course should not be changed by follies, the consequences of which, if the worst come to the worst, this country will have alike the power and, in case of need, the will to control. The State will, I trust, be ever careful to leave the domain of religious conscience free, and yet to keep it to its own domain; and to allow neither private caprice nor, above all, foreign arrogance to dictate to it in the discharge of its proper office. "England expects every man to do his duty;" and none can be so well prepared under all circumstances to exact its performance as that Liberal party, which has done the work of justice alike for Nonconformists and for Papal dissidents, and whose members have so often, for the sake of that work, hazarded their credit with the markedly Protestant constituencies of the country. Strong the State of the United Kingdom has always been in material strength; and its moral panoply is now, we may hope, pretty complete.

It is not then for the dignity of the Crown and people of the United Kingdom to be diverted from a path which they have deliberately chosen, and which it does not rest with all the myrmidons of the Apostolic Chamber either openly to obstruct, or secretly to undermine. It is rightfully to be expected, it is greatly to be desired, that the Roman Catholics of this country should do in the Nineteenth century what their forefathers of England, except a handful of emissaries, did in the Sixteenth, when they were marshalled in resistance to the Armada, and in the Seventeenth when, in despite of the Papal Chair, they sat in the House of Lords under the Oath of Allegiance. That which we are entitled to desire, we are entitled also to expect: indeed, to say we did not expect it, would, in my judgment, be the true way of conveying an "insult" to those concerned. In this expectation we may be partially disappointed. Should those to whom I appeal, thus unhappily come to bear witness in their own persons to the decay of sound, manly, true life in their Church, it will be their loss more than ours. The inhabitants of these Islands, as a whole, are

F

stable, though sometimes credulous and excitable;
resolute, though sometimes boastful : and a strong-
headed and soundhearted race will not be hindered,
either by latent or by avowed dissents, due to the
foreign influence of a caste, from the accomplish-
ment of its mission in the world.

APPENDICES.

APPENDIX A.

*The numbers here given correspond with those of the Eighteen Pro-
positions given in the text, where it would have been less convenient
to cite the originals.*

1, 2, 3. " Ex quâ omnino falsâ socialis regiminis ideâ haud
timent erroneam illam fovere opinionem, Catholicæ Ecclesiæ,
animarumque saluti maxime exitialem, a rec. mem. Gre-
gorio XIV. prædecessore Nostro *deliramentum* appellatam
(eâdem Encycl. ' Mirari '), nimirum, libertatem conscientiæ et
cultuum esse proprium cujuscunque hominis jus, quod lege
proclamari, et asseri debet in omni recte constitutâ societate,
et jus civibus inesse ad omnimodam libertatem nullâ vel
ecclesiasticâ, vel civili auctoritate coarctandam, quo suos
conceptus quoscumque sive voce sive typis, sive aliâ ratione
palam publiceque manifestare ac declarare valeant."—*Encyclical Letter.*

4. " Atque silentio præterire non possumus eorum auda-
ciam, qui sanam non sustinentes doctrinam ' illis Apostolicæ
Sedis judiciis, et decretis, quorum objectum ad bonum gene-

rale Ecclesiæ, ejusdemque jura, ac disciplinam spectare decla-
ratur, dummodo fidei morumque dogmata non attingat, posse
assensum et obedientiam detrectari absque peccato, et absque
ullâ Catholicæ professionis jacturâ.'"—*Ibid.*

5. "Ecclesia non est vera perfectaque societas plane libera,
nec pollet suis propriis et constantibus juribus sibi a divino
suo Fundatore collatis, sed civilis potestatis est definire quæ
sint Ecclesiæ jura, ac limites, intra quos eadem jura exercere
queat."—*Syllabus* v.

6. "Romani Pontifices et Concilia œcumenica a limiti-
bus suæ potestatis recesserunt, jura Principum usurpârunt,
atque etiam in rebus fidei et morum definiendis errârunt."—
Ibid. xxiii.

7. "Ecclesia vis inferendæ potestatem non habet, neque
potestatem ullam temporalem directam vel indirectam."—
Ibid. xxiv.

8. "Præter potestatem episcopatui inhærentem, alia est
attributa temporalis potestas a civili imperio vel expressè vel
tacitè concessa, revocanda propterea, cum libuerit, a civili
imperio."—*Ibid.* xxv.

9. "Ecclesiæ et personarum ecclesiasticarum immunitas a
jure civili ortum habuit."—*Ibid.* xxx.

10. "In conflictu legum utriusque potestatis, jus civile
prævalet."—*Ibid.* xlii.

11. "Catholicis viris probari potest ea juventutis insti-
tuendæ ratio, quæ sit a Catholicâ fide et ab Ecclesiæ potestate
sejuncta, quæque rerum dumtaxat, naturalium scientiam ac
terrenæ socialis vitæ fines tantummodo vel saltem primarium
spectet."—*Ibid.* xlviii.

12. "Philosophicarum rerum morumque scientia, itemque
civiles leges possunt et debent a divinâ et ecclesiasticâ auctoritate declinare."—*Ibid.* lvii.

13. "Matrimonii sacramentum non est nisi contractui acces-
sorium ab eoque separabile, ipsumque sacramentum in unâ
tantum nuptiali benedictione situm est."—*Ibid.* lxvi.

" Vi contractûs mere civilis potest inter Christianos con-
stare veri nominis matrimonium ; falsumque est, aut contractum matrimonii inter Christianos semper esse sacramentum,
aut nullum esse contractum, si sacramentum excludatur."
—*Ibid.* lxxiii.

14. " De temporalis regni cum spirituali compatibilitate
disputant inter se Christianæ et Catholicæ Ecclesiæ filii."—
Syllabus lxxv.

15. "Abrogatio civilis imperii, quo Apostolica Sedes poti-
tur, ad Ecclesiæ libertatem felicitatemque vel maxime con-
duceret."—*Ibid.* lxxvi.

16. " Ætate hac nostra non amplius expedit religionem
Catholicam haberi tanquam unicam status religionem, cæteris
quibuscumque cultibus exclusis."—*Ibid.* lxxvii.

17. "Hinc laudabiliter in quibusdam Catholici nominis
regionibus lege cautum est, ut hominibus illuc immigrantibus
liceat publicum proprii cujusque cultus exercitium habere."
—*Ibid.* lxxviii.

18. " Romanus Pontifex potest ac debet cum progressu,
cum liberalismo et cum recenti civilitate sese reconciliare et
componere."—*Ibid.* lxxx.

APPENDIX B.

I have contented myself with a minimum of citation from
the documents of the period before Emancipation. Their full
effect can only be gathered by such as are acquainted with,
or will take the trouble to refer largely to the originals. It
is worth while, however, to cite the following passage from
Bishop Doyle, as it may convey, through the indignation it
expresses, an idea of the amplitude of the assurances which
had been (as I believe, most honestly and sincerely) given.

" There is no justice, my Lord, in thus condemning us.

Such conduct on the part of our opponents creates in our bosoms a sense of wrong being done to us; it exhausts our patience, it provokes our indignation, and prevents us from reiterating our efforts to obtain a more impartial hearing. We are tempted, in such cases as these, to attribute unfair motives to those who differ from us, as we cannot conceive how men gifted with intelligence can fail to discover truths so plainly demonstrated as,

"That our faith or our allegiance is not regulated by any such doctrines as those imputed to us;

"That our duties to the Government of our country are not influenced nor affected by any Bulls or practices of Popes;

"That these duties are to be learned by us, as by every other class of His Majesty's subjects, from the Gospel, from the reason given to us by God, from that love of country which nature has implanted in our hearts, and from those constitutional maxims, which are as well understood, and as highly appreciated, by Catholics of the present day, as by their ancestors, who founded them with Alfred, or secured them at Runnymede."—*Doyle's ' Essay on the Catholic Claims,'* London, 1826, p. 38.

The same general tone, as in 1826, was maintained in the answers of the witnesses from Maynooth College before the Commission of 1855. See, for example, pp. 132, 161–4, 272–3, 275, 361, 370–5, 381–2, 394–6, 405. The Commission reported (p. 64), "We see no reason to believe that there has been any disloyalty in the teaching of the College, or any disposition to impair the obligations of an unreserved allegiance to your Majesty.'

APPENDIX C.

Compare the recent and ominous forecasting of the future European policy of the British Crown, in an Article from a Romish Periodical for the current month, which has direct relation to these matters, and which has every appearance of proceeding from authority.

"Surely in any European complication, such as may any day arise, nay, such as must ere long arise, from the natural gravitation of the forces, which are for the moment kept in check and truce by the necessity of preparation for their inevitable collision, it may very well be that the future prosperity of England may be staked in the struggle, and that the side which she may take may be determined, not either by justice or interest, but *by a passionate resolve to keep up the Italian kingdom at any hazard.*"—The '*Month*' for November, 1874: 'Mr. Gladstone's Durham Letter,' p. 265.

This is a remarkable disclosure. With *whom* could England be brought into conflict by any disposition she might feel to keep up the Italian kingdom? Considered as States, both Austria and France are in complete harmony with Italy. But it is plain that Italy has some enemy; and the writers of the 'Month' appear to know who it is.

APPENDIX D.

Notice has been taken, both in this country and abroad, of the apparent inertness of public men, and of at least one British Administration, with respect to the subject of these pages. See Friedberg, 'Gränzen zwischen Staat und Kirche,' Abtheilung iii. pp. 755–6; and the Preface to the Fifth Volume of Mr. Greenwood's elaborate, able, and judicial work, entitled 'Cathedra Petri,' p. iv.

"If there be any chance of such a revival, it would become

our political leaders to look more closely into the peculiarities of a system, which denies the right of the subject to freedom of thought and action upon matters most material to his civil and religious welfare. There is no mode of ascertaining the spirit and tendency of great institutions but in a careful study of their history. The writer is profoundly impressed with the conviction that our political instructors have wholly neglected this important duty : or, which is perhaps worse, left it in the hands of a class of persons whose zeal has outrun their discretion, and who have sought rather to engage the prejudices than the judgment of their hearers in the cause they have, no doubt sincerely, at heart."

Page 20.—(*a*) " Therefore do We, by our Apostolic authority, repudiate, proscribe, and condemn, all and each of the evil opinions and doctrines severally mentioned in this Letter, and We will and order that they be absolutely held, by all the children of the Catholic Church, to be repudiated, proscribed, and condemned."

Page 33.—(*b*) " This most holy, ecumenical, and general Tridentine Synod, in the Holy Ghost regularly assembled, and having for Presidents the three aforesaid Apostolic Legates, exhorts, *or* teaches, *or* determines, *or* decrees."

(*c*) " The Canons and Decrees of the most holy ecumenical Council of Trent."

Page 34.—(*d*) " Pius, Bishop, servant of the servants of God."

(*e*) " We teach and define it to be a dogma divinely revealed that, when the Roman Pontiff speaks *ex cathedrâ*, that is when, in discharge of the office of Pastor and Teacher of all Christians, by virtue of his supreme Apostolic authority, he defines that a doctrine regarding faith or morals is to be held by the Universal Church, he enjoys, by the Divine assistance promised to him in blessed Peter, that infallibility with which the Divine Redeemer willed His Church to be endowed in defining a doctrine regarding faith or morals; and that therefore such definitions of the Roman Pontiff are irreformable of themselves, and not from the consent of the Church."—*Taken from the version in 'Dogmatic Contributions.'* Dublin : O'Toole. 1870.

Page 37.—(*f*) " To be believed and held by all the faithful."

Page 38.—(*g*) " All, both pastors and faithful, of whatsoever rite and dignity, both individually and collectively, are bound to submit, by the duty of hierarchical subordination and true obedience, not only in matters belonging to faith and morals, but also in those that appertain to the discipline and government of the Church throughout the world. . . . This is the teaching of the Catholic Faith, from which no one can deviate without detriment to faith and salvation." *Ibid.* (But I consider the word detriment to be much too weak : for the deviation is made the subject of Anathema at the end of the chapter.) . . . " We further teach and declare, that he (the Pope) is the supreme Judge of the Faithful, and that, in all causes [appertaining to ecclesiastical jurisdiction], recourse may be had to his judgment; and that none may reopen the judgment of the Apostolic See, than whose there is no greater authority ; and that it is not lawful for any one to sit in judgment on its judgment." *Ibid.* But for the words in brackets I should substitute " of ecclesiastical cognisance."

Page 41.—(*h*) " Not only in matters belonging to faith and morals, but also in those that appertain to the discipline and government of the Church throughout the world." *Ibid.*

LONDON : PRINTED BY WILLIAM CLOWES AND SONS, STAMFORD STREET AND CHARING CROSS.